BUNNIES

as pets

---◆---

**A GUIDE TO THE SELECTION,
CARE AND BREEDING OF
RABBITS.**

---◆---

illustrated by
THREE LIONS, INC.

ISBN 0-87666-187-8

Distributed in the U.S.A. by T.F.H. Publications, Inc., 211 West Sylvania Avenue, P.O. Box 27, Neptune City, N.J. 07753; in England by T.F.H. (Gt. Britain) Ltd., 13 Nutley Lane, Reigate, Surrey; in Canada to the book store and library trade by Clarke, Irwin & Company, Clarwin House, 791 St. Clair Avenue West, Toronto 10, Ontario; in Canada to the pet trade by Rolf C. Hagen Ltd., 3225 Sartelon Street, Montreal 382, Quebec; in Southeast Asia by Y.W. Ong, 9 Lorong 36 Geylang, Singapore 14; in Australia and the south Pacific by Pet Imports Pty. Ltd., P.O. Box 149, Brookvale 2100, N.S.W., Australia. Published by T.F.H. Publications, Inc. Ltd., The British Crown Colony of Hong Kong.

This booklet is dedicated to Mr. O. Tutwiler,
Tampa, Florida. He raises better rabbits -
though fewer- than anyone else I know.
M.M.

Babies and bunnies!!

INTRODUCTION

The rabbit has been a pet and a laboratory animal for a good many years. They are playful and very tame when young and though they can never be housebroken (there are exceptions), their cleanliness is really astounding. As you may or may not know, rabbits have been developed with many interesting and varied colors and coats. The chart based on the standards of the American Rabbit and Cavy Breeders Association, 5941 Baum Boulevard, Pittsburgh 6, Pennsylvania, gives some idea of the enormous variability of this wonderful pet.

By far the most popular variety is the white albino rabbit. So popular is this race of bunny that millions are sold as pets around Easter time. This booklet is intended for the beginner. It will give you the fundamentals in keeping and breeding your rabbit.

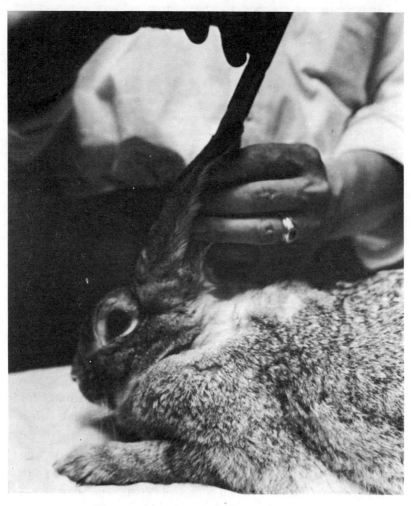

A good rabbit, regardless of the type, must have long ears. The better the rabbit, the longer the ears. Don't use the ears for handles!

A LIST OF THE MORE COMMON RABBIT BREEDS USED FOR LABORATORY PURPOSES AND THEIR OUTSTANDING CHARACTERISTICS BASED ON STANDARDS OF THE AMERICAN RABBIT AND CAVY BREEDERS ASSOCIATION *

Breed	Adult Body Weight (pounds) ♂ ♀	Ear Length (inches)	Colors	Phenotype	Type	Bone	Distinctive Characters
English Angora	5-7	3-4	Albino	cc	Cobby, compact	Medium small	Long hair
French Angora	7-8	4½	Albino	cc	Medium long	Medium	Long hair
California	8-9	4½	White, black extremities	$c^H c^H$	Medium long	Small	
Champagne de Argents	9-11 9½-12	4½-5	Silver, black undercolor		Medium	Small	Breadth
Cream de Argents	9 10	4½-5	Silver, yellow undercolor		Medium	Small	Breadth
Checkered Giants	11+ 12+	6	Black, Blue	$Enaa$ $Enaadd$		Medium	Colored spots on white background
Belgian Hares	8	5	Gray, agouti	Aww	Long, racy	Fine	Body type
Viennas	9-10 10-11	5	Blue	$aadd$	Heavy-weight, cobby	Medium	
Beveren	9 10	5	Blue, White	$aadd$ $aaddw$	Tapering, mandolin	Heavy	Blue eyes
Chinchilla	6-7½ 6¼-8	4½	Gray, agouti	Ach^3	Medium long, chubby	Medium	Fur quality
Dutch	4½	3½	Varied	$du^d du^w$		Medium	White belt
English	6-8	4	Varied	En		Medium	Colored spots
Flemish	14+ 15+	6-6½	Varied	Varied	Long	Heavy	Size
Havana	6	3¾-4	Chocolate brown	$aabb$	Cobby	Medium fine	
Himalayan	3½	3½	White, black extremities	$c^H c^H$	Snaky		Markings
Lops	10 11	8-9	Varied		Heavy	Heavy	Ear length
New Zealand	9-11 10-12	4-5½	Red or white	ee or cc	Blocky	Medium	
Polish	2¼ 2¾	2¼-2½	White or colored	cc or C	Short	Fine	Small size
Rex	7 7½	4-4½	Varied	$r^1 r^1$	Blocky	Medium	Short hair

* 5941 Baum Blvd., Pittsburgh 6, Pa.

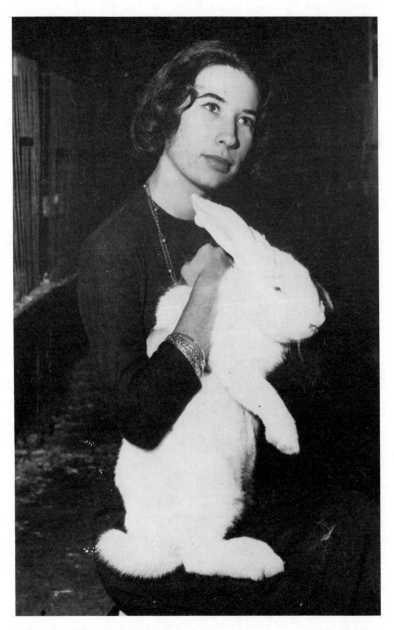

When purchasing a rabbit or making arrangements for its housing, remember that the animal you buy is going to grow and grow fast, so plan accordingly—don't assume that the housing quarters for a baby rabbit will be comfortable for an adult.

Rabbits like plenty of air and cleanliness in their homes.

HOUSING YOUR PET RABBIT

The primary consideration in housing your pet rabbit is cleanliness. You can easily obtain a special rabbit cage from your pet shop, or you can improvise with an orange crate in which you've made a wire screen door. Rabbits are great chewers, so be careful that your pet doesn't bite his way out of the cage. Put some torn newspapers on the bottom of the cage and change these every day or so if you keep the box indoors.

There are many different breeds; some are bred primarily as fur producers or meat producers, and others are bred primarily as pets and exhibition animals. Here a prize-winning Netherland Dwarf poses with just a few of its trophies. Photo by John E. Williams.

If you can maintain your pet rabbit outside (don't worry about him getting cold as they are very hardy), then the job is that much easier. Be certain that your pet cannot escape, or you will have a tough job finding him again.

HANDLING YOUR PET RABBIT

So many people are under the impression that because a rabbit has large ears they should be used as handles! Nothing could be further from the truth. A rabbit has very sensitive ears and they do not appreciate being picked up by them. When you do pick up a rabbit by the ears you are taking the

This is the proper way to hold a rabbit.

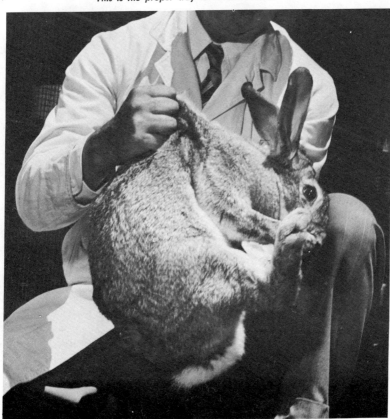

Bedecked in Easter finery or entirely unadorned, a pet rabbit is an appealing, interesting animal capable of feeling pain. It deserves good care and should not be treated as a toy that can be neglected and discarded at will. Photo by Michelin.

Training your rabbit is fun . . . it can be done!

chance of getting scratched, as the rabbit doesn't feel too
secure this way and starts to kick.

Pick up the rabbit about the body, as though he were a
dog. Place your hand over his shoulders and around the sides
of his front legs. With your other hand lift up his rear. Use
two hands in holding the rabbit and given the proper balance,
he will remain motionless.

Notice the profuse vegetative growth under this wire-bottomed hutch. Rabbit droppings that fall through the wire bottom are especially rich in plant nutrients. Photo by Louise Boyle.

Dogs and rabbits can get along fine.

Normally, rabbits don't bite, but they have the equipment to do so. Their front teeth are ever-growing and require hard, chewy substances to keep them worn down. Keep that in mind!

It is perfectly permissible to allow your child to play with the bunny as much as he wants, but be certain that he understands that the rabbit is a living thing and not to be treated like a stuffed toy.

Even with gross mishandling, it is a very rare occurrence that a bunny will nip.

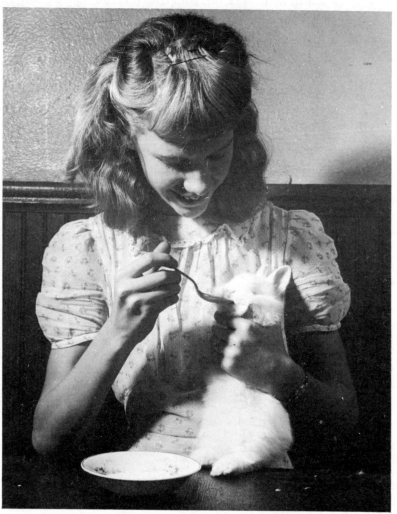

If your rabbit needs vitamins, give them to him with a spoon.

FEEDING YOUR RABBIT

The digestive system of the rabbit is a very long one running from 20 to 26 feet in length. This means that the rabbit is adapted for eating huge quantities of low nutritive value food. The inside of the digestive system is so constructed as to insure that every bit of nutritive matter can be utilized. In nature the rabbit consumes large amounts of fresh or dried grasses, grains, weeds, vegetables and the like. Rabbits do best on these natural foods, but there are some very excellent substitutes available at your pet shop in the

Rabbit pellets are excellent rabbit food.

A family of New Zealand Whites curiously
inspecting the view from an open cage.
Photo by Stemo.

Don't try to feed your rabbit while you are holding him.

form of rabbit pellets. These pellets are compressed greens (usually lettuce, alfalfa, etc.). They are better than the raw greens because they keep longer, are easier to feed, are cleaner, they do not contain parasites which might infect your bunny, and they are cheap! By the way, if you so desire, it is perfectly alright to offer carrots to your rabbit. They love them and the carrots are nutritious. Don't feed them carrots more than twice a week though or you might have them refuse to eat other foods.

Offer the food in a crock made of earthenware. A pottery dog dish is very suitable. Metal pans serve well but the rabbit might tip them if they are light in weight. The rabbit likes water too, so offer plenty of water . . . they are heavy drinkers. Water can be served in the same earthenware dishes as the food, or you can make (or purchase) a waterbottle. The waterbottle is merely a large bottle fitted with a plug. In the plug is a metal or glass nipple which releases the water when the rabbit sucks on the end of it. This method is by far the best as sanitation is insured. Change the water every day if you use an open dish.

A good meat rabbit weighs 15 or 16 pounds.

TRAINING YOUR RABBIT

The rabbit is a very difficult animal to train, though it is a very easy animal to tame. As a matter of fact, when you purchase your rabbit it is probably already tamed for you.

Many people like to train their rabbits to a harness and lead so their children can take them outside without any fear of them running off and getting lost. This is easily done, though you shouldn't expect that the rabbit will walk as comfortably on the end of a lead as a dog would.

Be content with a tame rabbit that comes to you when you offer it some food. If possible get a young bunny. The older a rabbit is the tougher it is to tame.

A rabbit is equipped to be nasty . . . but they rarely are. Their teeth must be worn down by chewing or the rabbit will die from too much tooth growth.

Breed rabbits for a purpose. If you want meat, raise big rabbits;
if you want pets or laboratory animals, raise albinos.

BREEDING YOUR RABBIT

The rabbit is a very interesting animal to breed. The doe ovulates only after copulation with a male; this practically insures fertilization. This peculiar aspect of rabbit reproduction has made it popular as a laboratory animal because it is then possible to time fertilization within an hour.

Breeding rabbits for pets or for food is a relatively easy process and is usually accomplished with little effort. Most people merely put the male and female adult together and in no time at all they have baby rabbits.

Breeding cages should be so constructed that you can easily view what is going on inside.

Does do not always show an interest in the male. At one time it was thought that the female was in constant 'season', but this proved to be erroneous. The cycle of the female rabbit is about 15 or 16 days. There are outward signs of receptivity in the female (such as the swollen, purple vulva), and a noticeable restlessness, nervousness and rubbing of the head and body against the cage, are signs that the female will be receptive to the male.

The gestation period of the female is about one month (28-36 days), though this figure varies with the race (variety). Sexual maturity also varies with the race and some rabbits are mature sexually at four months of age (the large Flemish rabbits are not mature for close to a year). Interestingly enough, accurate records of parturition terminating some 3500 pregnancies show that about 7 out of 10 litters are born between daybreak and noon; less than 1 out of 10 are born during the hours of darkness!

The newborn rabbits may be handled at birth and they may even be transferred to foster mothers within the first 48 hours of birth. Young rabbits are nursed for about two months (from 6 to 8 weeks), though the mother usually begins to dry up after 6 weeks and they are usually all dry by the eighth week. The rabbit is so hardy that she may be bred immediately after her youngsters are two months old.

Experimental laboratories are usually capable of taking the young rabbits from their mothers at an early age, weaning them artificially. When this is done the female rabbit may be bred as early as two weeks after parturition. It is not advisable to force breed the female more than two or three times. The fourth or fifth litter usually shows signs of overbreeding. A litter of rabbits may run as high as nine bunnies!

In general, if you are interested in breeding a large number of rabbits, it will be wiser to separate the sexes. When the female is ready to breed she should be placed into the male's pen. If you place the male in with the female you are gambling with the life of the buck.

Mating should occur in a very short time if the male is virile and the doe is receptive. The mating is successful if the buck falls on his side during coitus. One mating is sufficient to insure fertilization and the female should be removed after copulation has been completed. The female will mate during her entire period of pregnancy, though only one contact was actually necessary.

These Angorra beauties are on their way to getting a haircut.

False pregnancies in rabbits are very common and it is possible that two female rabbits may be able to induce ovulation in each other, thus setting off the cycle which will result in false pregnancy. The doe will breed with a male after the onset of false pregnancy but she will be sterile for the whole 16 day cycle. Artificial insemination is very easy in rabbits and the semen of the male may be stored for a week at 55°F.

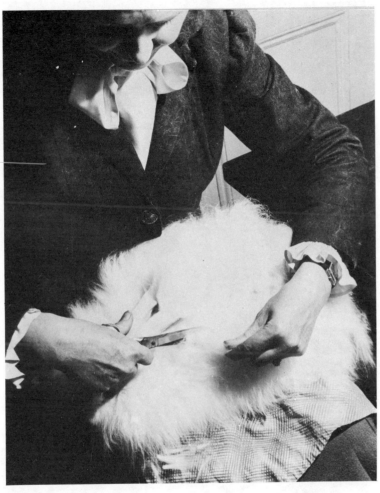

Giving the Angorra rabbit a haircut is a very profitable venture.

Higher or lower temperatures greatly reduce the longevity of the sperm.

Breeding is best accomplished in the spring if the rabbits are kept outdoors. In some races, the female will remain nonreceptive during the cold winter months . . . in other races they will breed all year round.

A nest of young rabbits in the wild. Photo by American Museum of Natural History.

Enough fur for two Angorra sweaters!

DISEASES OF RABBITS

Disease in any animal must be considered, and it goes without saying that 'An ounce of prevention is worth a pound of cure!' The greatest menace to a caged rabbit is filth and unless the cage is kept fairly clean you can expect to have problems. If your rabbit is properly fed and properly cleaned you can look forward to a disease-free and hardy pet.

Just in case you should have health problems, the following summary may be of value to you.

DISEASES OF THE SKIN

EAR CANKER is caused by small little bugs called mites. If your rabbit has ear canker it will always be shaking its head and scratching its ears. The base of the ear will have

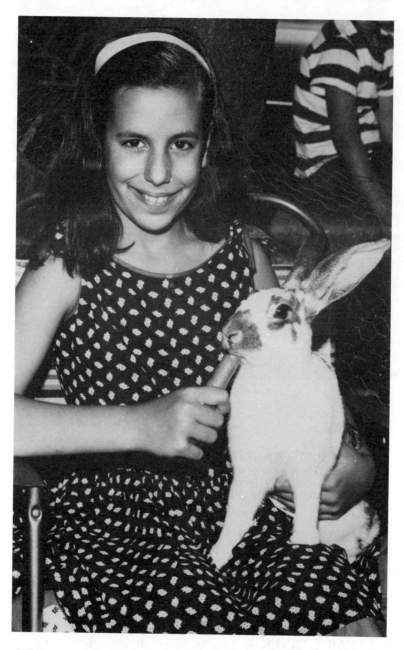

Children and rabbits can mix well—provided that a young owner is carefully coached and supervised in living up to the responsibilities of ownership.

red, yellow or whitish scales on the skin surface. Your pet shop can supply you with dog or cat ear canker medicine and you should use it as directed. If you catch ear canker in its early stages, just apply a few drops of vegetable oil to the area. Repeat this for a week and if the canker doesn't clear up then call in your veterinarian.

An Angorra after the trimming!

Check your rabbit's ears for canker. Give the rabbit a general physical checkup as often as possible. All the drugs are just gimmicks which the model used for posing.

SKIN MANGE is also caused by mites. The rabbit will always be scratching itself about the infected area until finally all the hair about the infected part has been worn away. As the disease progresses there will be a yellowish crusty scab formed due to the constant scratching and tearing of the skin. Clip the hair from around the infected area and wash with a mild disinfectant soap. Then apply a mange medicine available from your pet shop. Dog mange medicine works very well. A home remedy of 1 part flower of sulphur and 3 parts lard is considered very helpful.

RINGWORM is caused by several parasites. It affects the rabbit similarly to skin mange but on a close examination you will notice that the patches of skin which are scaly have red 'goosepimples'. The ringworm infection usually starts on the head or on the feet. Clip and wash the area as though you were treating mange. Then swab the entire area with tincture of iodine. Get some ringworm medicine from your pet shop and apply this too.

Rabbits are sold and bred for their use as laboratory animals. They command a nice price too, so if you have excess stock you can contact your local hospital and sell them.

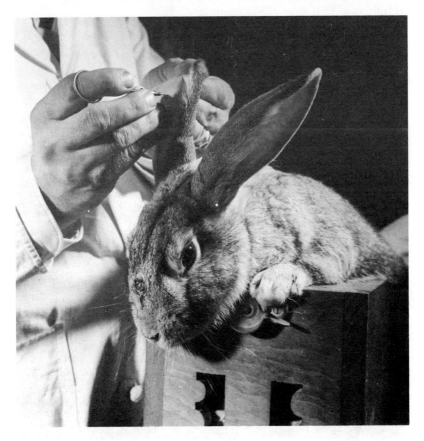

RESPIRATORY DISEASES

Cold or sniffles is a common symptom. The rabbit sniffles and sneezes just like a human being with a cold. Give the animal rest and exercise. Allow the rabbit to bask in the sun, if at all possible. Feed carrots and more nutritious foods.

Sometimes pneumonia might develop in very young rabbits or in nursing does. If this happens your rabbit will lose its appetite and be very thirsty, fighting the high body temperature. The breathing will be labored and heavy. If you catch it before the diarrhea starts you should give the animal a shot of penicillin (through your vet) or some other suitable antibiotic (Terramycin, Auromycin, etc.).

Other diseases of the rabbit are so complicated and rare that they are not worth mentioning in this small booklet. If your rabbit is very ill call in your veterinarian and see what the trouble is.

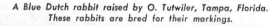
*A Blue Dutch rabbit raised by O. Tutwiler, Tampa, Florida.
These rabbits are bred for their markings.*